TIME

MANAGING EDITOR Richard Stengel
ART DIRECTOR Arthur Hochstein

Ted Kennedy: A Tribute

EDITOR Richard Lacayo
DESIGNER D.W. Pine
PICTURE EDITOR Crary Pullen
ASSOCIATE EDITOR Deirdre van Dyk
ASSOCIATE PICTURE EDITOR Deirdre Read
EDITORIAL PRODUCTION Lionel P. Vargas

TIME INC. HOME ENTERTAINMENT

PUBLISHER Richard Fraiman
GENERAL MANAGER Steven Sandonato
EXECUTIVE DIRECTOR, MARKETING SERVICES Carol Pittard
DIRECTOR, RETAIL & SPECIAL SALES Tom Mifsud
DIRECTOR, NEW PRODUCT DEVELOPMENT Peter Harper
ASSISTANT DIRECTOR, BOOKAZINE MARKETING Laura Adam
ASSISTANT PUBLISHING DIRECTOR, BRAND MARKETING Joy Butts
ASSOCIATE COUNSEL Helen Wan
BOOK PRODUCTION MANAGER Suzanne Janso
DESIGN & PREPRESS MANAGER Anne-Michelle Gallero
ASSOCIATE BRAND MANAGER Michela Wilde

SPECIAL THANKS TO:

Christine Austin, Beth Bland, Glenn Buonocore, Jim Childs, Susan Chodakiewicz, Rose Cirrincione, Jacqueline Fitzgerald, Lauren Hall, Jennifer Jacobs, Brynn Joyce, Mona Li, Robert Marasco, Amy Migliaccio, Richard Prue, Brooke Reger, Dave Rozzelle, Andrea Sachs, Carolyn Sayre, Ilene Schreider, Adriana Tierno, TIME Copy Desk, TIME Imaging, Alex Voznesenskiy, Sydney Webber

Copyright © 2009 Time Inc. Home Entertainment
Published by TIME Books, Time Inc. • 1271 Avenue of the Americas • New York, N.Y. 10020

ISBN 13: 978-1-60320-125-4
ISBN 10: 1-60320-125-4
Library of Congress Number: 2009931981

We welcome your comments and suggestions about TIME Books. Please write to us at:
TIME Books, Attention: Book Editors, P.O. Box 11016, Des Moines, Iowa 50336-1016

If you would like to order any of our hardcover Collector's Edition books,
please call us at 1-800-327-6388
(Monday through Friday, 7 a.m.–8 p.m., or Saturday, 7 a.m.–6 p.m., C.T.)

Campaigning for re-election in 1970, Kennedy greets a crowd in Boston

Contents

Ted's Lasting Legacy

FOR MORE THAN A HALF-CENTURY, the Kennedy family has had a grip on the collective consciousness of Americans. Its members' lives have always seemed to require from us words like *fate, destiny* and *tragedy*. By the magnitude of their ambitions, achievements and misfortunes, they made the already tumultuous times they lived in seem even larger.

In all of that, Edward Kennedy was truly a member of the Kennedy clan—large in his strengths, his energies, his goals and even sometimes his weaknesses. Because he was a Kennedy, it was probably inevitable that Ted would enter public life. What was not inevitable was that he would distinguish himself there. But he did. During almost five decades in the Senate, Kennedy was the nation's most tireless defender of the poor and the powerless. He left his mark on the largest issues of our time, including civil rights, immigration, education, the fight against AIDS and the decades-long struggle to provide decent health care to all Americans. His elder brothers John and Robert made the Kennedy name exciting and inspiring. Ted made it enduring.

This book chronicles Kennedy's life in words and pictures, from his beginnings as the youngest child of Joe and Rose Kennedy to his final years, when he was the third-longest-serving member of the Senate (behind only Robert Byrd of West Virginia and Strom Thurmond of South Carolina). It was a life that took him from Harvard and Hyannis Port to Washington, through the trauma of the Kennedy assassinations, the tragedy of Chappaquiddick, the disappointment of his failed bid for the presidency and the renewed vigor of his Senate career. We see him as a grinning little boy, a strapping football player, a political campaigner who never lost a race, a brother grieving for a lost brother, a devoted father and uncle, and the hardworking lawmaker who become the Lion of the Senate.

Though there are some prominent members of the next generation of Kennedys, with the passing of Ted—the youngest and last of Joe's boys—a major chapter of the Kennedy saga has drawn to a close. We tend to think of American history in terms of Presidents. Abraham Lincoln, Teddy Roosevelt, Franklin D. Roosevelt, Ronald Reagan—all of them appear to us as figures who shaped the times in which they lived. Senators aren't often remembered in the same large way. But we know at least one who almost certainly will be. This book is about him.

from the EDITORS OF TIME

Setting Sail in Life

Young Ted, age 6, launching a toy sailboat in 1938, was the most gregarious and outgoing member of the family. But with eight siblings, he still had to fight to be heard

Camera-Ready

Ted lived for a time in London while his father was U.S. ambassador to Britain. With sister Jean, far right, he waits to capture the changing of the guard at Buckingham Palace

Boy Overboard

Sailing was so important to the family that eldest brother Joe, rear, once dumped Ted, front, into the water when he failed to correctly identify the jib

Big Brother
Because of their 17-year age gap, Joe Jr., with Ted in 1941, was almost a father figure, urging his brother to put his nose to the grindstone at school

Team Player

At 6 ft. 2 in. and 200 lb., Ted, far right, like his brothers before him, was a fierce competitor, earning a varsity letter in his senior year at Harvard

Taking Off

Joan and Ted make ready to sail in July 1959, about the time Ted was preparing to take the bar exam

Wedding Belle

Joan met Ted when he dedicated a gym at her college. The shy musician and the gregarious law student emerge from their wedding in 1958, with best man J.F.K.

The Youngest Brother

by TED SORENSEN

WHEN I FIRST MET TED KENNEDY 55 years ago, he did not initially seem to be much more than "the kid brother"—fun, funny, friendly, but not a major part of the genial Kennedy dinner-table conversations on policy and politics. When I last met with him, in the summer of 2008, he was the Senate's next-to-eldest statesman convening a breakfast meeting to discuss his plan to establish a research institute or foundation for the scholarly study of the Senate, its role and history in American public life. I took that opportunity to present to him a copy of my new book of memoirs, *Counselor: A Life at the Edge of History,* with a personal inscription commending him on his accomplishments and predicting more in an even brighter future. In a few days, he graciously replied to my letter and closed with a prediction that an Obama victory would implement my ideals.

"Kid brother" to senior statesman has been an extraordinary journey, matching the similar journeys taken by his brothers John and Robert. All three of the Kennedy brothers who entered our national public life—meaning the three who survived World War II—demonstrated this extraordinary quality of growth, particularly after they arrived in Washington. Too many successful politicians stop growing once they reach there, certain that they already know it all and have already completed their growth within the biblical standard of "wisdom and stature, and in favor with God and Man." But not the Kennedys, and certainly not Edward Moore Kennedy. A Harvard education; a University of Virginia law degree; a stint as an assistant district attorney in Boston; a key role in managing Jack's Senate re-election campaign in 1958; and equally key assignments in J.F.K.'s successful contest for the Democratic presidential nomination in 1960

The three brothers in Hyannis Port in 1948, top; right, in 1960, after J.F.K. won the Democratic nomination

and his successful race to win the presidency—all contributed to Ted's rise in the esteem of his brothers and their respective staff, including me. Through each of those phases, "Teddy" was growing, maturing, developing, learning and gaining new experience and insights.

Spurred by his father and by his own interests to seek the Senate seat for Massachusetts that J.F.K. had vacated upon entering the White House, Teddy entered a hotly contested Democratic primary in 1962. He was opposed—to President Kennedy's consternation—by Eddie McCormack, the favorite nephew of the House Democratic majority leader John McCormack of South Boston. President Kennedy, whose brother Bob was then serving as Attorney General, was concerned that he would be accused of fostering nepotism and founding a dynasty. He did not wish to add a feud with Eddie's uncle to his already difficult relations with Congress. Neither did he wish to add still another private disagreement with his beloved father to an already long list. So he publicly vowed that the White House would remain neutral regarding the 1962 Senate Democratic nomination in Massachusetts. But privately he asked R.F.K. and me to fly unannounced to Cape Cod and brief Teddy on the eve of his first televised debate with young McCormack. We did, in a dining-table session not unlike those I held with J.F.K. to brief him before his first televised debate with Nixon and later to prep him for his biweekly press conferences as President. We found Teddy surprisingly relaxed and informed. He won the debate, the primary and the election, just as he has won every race for re-election in the 47 years since.

The pride and joy that all three brothers felt in serving in high national office at the same time was cut short by their father's stroke in 1961 and by Jack's assassination in November 1963. Through the difficult years that followed, Teddy's growth continued. Both a plane crash in Massachusetts in 1964 and the ugly automobile accident on Chappaquiddick Island in 1969 almost cost him his life; and the Chappaquiddick incident ultimately ended his bright prospects for still higher office.

And yet Teddy never lost his drive to serve his country and honor his brothers' memory. Bobby's assassination left Teddy in charge of not only the Kennedy legacy but the Kennedy family as well. Already a loving father of his own wonderful children, he took special care to help guide and comfort Jack's and Bobby's survivors. Throughout it all, his impact as a Senator and a Democratic Party leader continued. He worked well with friends across the aisle, whether the Democrats were in the minority or majority, building relationships with Presidents of both parties, including L.B.J. (when R.F.K. did not) and Carter (who did not reciprocate). Fellow Senators on more than one occasion have told me that when Ted rose on the Senate floor to speak, members of both parties paid attention whether or not their views were compatible with his, because they knew he had done his homework. He gained a reputation for first-rate staffers, and I can testify to their uniform excellence, including those in his Senate office and on the Senate Judiciary Committee. One example of the latter was Stephen Breyer, now a Justice of the Supreme Court. For years, Ted's aides on media relations, speechwriting and other key assignments continued to love and serve him; and that low turnover guaranteed continued excellence.

He initially focused on domestic policies of particular importance to R.F.K., including health care, civil rights, immigration, education and other key issues. Always an internationalist who favored legal and diplomatic solutions supported by our allies to resolve international conflicts, he became in later years particularly outspoken against the war in Iraq. He did not shy away from taking the lead on controversial issues in the Senate, even those sensitive back home in

Displayed around the Senate reception room, the chamber where legislators meet their constituents, are nine portraits of distinguished Senators. Two spaces remain to be filled

Massachusetts—including school busing, women's reproductive rights and judicial nominations.

Having sat by his bedside to see him come back from both his near fatal plane crash and his automobile accident, I had hoped he would last another generation, dying at some dramatic moment on the Senate floor that he loved.

Several decades ago, John F. Kennedy, as a Senator known for his special interest in history—including particularly the history of the Senate itself—was named to head a special committee to select five Senators whose portraits would hang in the Senate reception room for all to see. "The Famous Five" were to be chosen on the basis of their historic contributions in terms of courage, integrity and substantive activity over a long Senate career. They are now called "The Famous Nine," after two Senate resolutions added four more portraits.

There are still two spaces remaining in that room. I can think of no one more deserving of having his portrait placed there now than Senator Edward M. Kennedy.

Sorensen was formerly the special counsel and adviser to President John F. Kennedy, and is the author of Counselor: A Life at the Edge of History

High Hopes
On an Election Day stop during the pivotal May 1960 West Virginia presidential primary, J.F.K. consults Ted, who had barnstormed around the state on his brother's behalf. J.F.K.'s landslide victory that day secured him the Democratic nomination

Watch and Wait

On the night of the 1960 presidential election, Ted and sister Pat are glued to the set at the family compound watching the returns. Ted spent much of the year running J.F.K.'s campaign in the Western states. The race was so close that Richard Nixon didn't concede until the next day

Local Hero

With his brother in the White House, Ted ran in 1962 for J.F.K.'s old Senate seat with the slogan "He can do more for Massachusetts." Here he campaigns on Labor Day weekend in Lawrence, Mass.

Fatal Accident

In a June 1964 plane crash that killed the pilot as well as Ted's aide Ed Moss, Kennedy suffered a broken back and was immobilized in a hospital for five months

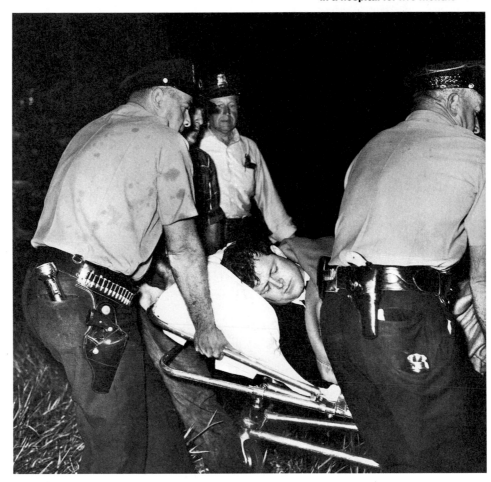

The Good Son

Teddy, the family jester, could make his stern mother laugh. He was so fond of this 1962 photograph, it hung for many years in his Senate office

American Tragedy
On Nov. 25, 1963, as J.F.K.'s funeral cortege moves down Connecticut Avenue, the surviving Kennedy brothers flank the President's widow Jacqueline

Fact-Finding Mission

**Kennedy's position on the
Vietnam War evolved gradually
throughout the 1960s. By
October 1965, when he made
this visit to a refugee camp in
Pleiku, South Vietnam, he was
beginning to have misgivings
about the conduct of the war and
the justifications for continuing it**

Derailed

On the morning of July 19, 1969, a pair of vacationing fishermen spotted Kennedy's overturned Oldsmobile in a Chappaquiddick tidal pond. They initially assumed it was just an abandoned car. Then a police diver arrived and discovered the body of Mary Jo Kopechne inside

Respite

After Bobby's assassination in June 1968, Ted, on the jetty near his Hyannis home in May 1969, became head of the family and father figure to 16 children

The Man In Full

by RICHARD LACAYO

THERE WAS A TIME 40 YEARS AGO, right after the assassination of his brother Robert, when it appeared that Edward Kennedy would become President someday by right of succession. The Kennedy curse, the one that had seen all three of his brothers cut down in their prime, had created for him a sort of Kennedy prerogative, or at least the illusion of one, an inevitable claim on the White House. For years he seemed like a man simply waiting for the right moment to take what everybody knew was coming his way.

Everybody was wrong. Ted Kennedy would never reach the White House. His weaknesses—and the long shadow of Chappaquiddick—were an obstacle that even his strengths couldn't overcome. But his failure to get to the presidency opened the way to the true fulfillment of his gifts, which was to become one of the greatest legislators in American history. When their White House years are over, most Presidents set off on the long aftermath of themselves. They give lectures, write books, play golf and make money. Jimmy Carter even won a Nobel Prize. But every one of them would tell you that elder-statesmanship is no substitute for real power.

Because Kennedy never made it to the finish line, he never had to endure a postpresidential twilight. Instead, he had 46 working years in Congress, time enough to leave his imprint on everything from the Voting Rights Act of 1965 to the Edward M. Kennedy Serve America Act of 2009, a law that expands support for national community-service programs. Over the years, Kennedy was a force behind the Freedom of Information Act, the Occupational Safety and Health Act, and the Americans with Disabilities Act. He helped Soviet dissidents and fought apartheid. Above all, he conducted a four-decade crusade for universal health coverage. Along

Edward Kennedy in 2000 in his Washington offices

the way, he vastly expanded the network of neighborhood clinics, virtually invented the COBRA system for portable insurance and helped create the laws that provide Medicare prescriptions and family leave.

And for most of that time, he went forward against great odds, the voice of progressivism in a conservative age. When people were getting tired of hearing about racism or the poor or the decay of American cities, he kept talking. When liberalism was flickering, there was Kennedy, holding the torch, insisting that "we can light those beacon fires again." In the last year of his life, with the Inauguration of Barack Obama, he had the satisfaction of seeing a big part of that dream fulfilled. In early 2008, when Obama had just begun to capture the public imagination, Kennedy bucked the party establishment. Just before Super Tuesday, the venerable Senator from Massachusetts enthusiastically endorsed the young Senator from Illinois, helping propel Obama to the Democratic nomination and ultimately the White House.

So does it matter that Kennedy never made it to the presidency? Any number of mere Presidents have been pretty much forgotten. But as the Romans understood, there can be Emperors of no consequence—and Senators whose legacies are carved in stone.

R OSE KENNEDY WANTED A FAMILY. Joe Kennedy wanted a dynasty. They both got what they wanted, but only for a time. The elder Kennedys came from Irish-American families that had fought their way up in a Boston society run by an Anglophile Wasp aristocracy that held the Irish in contempt. Rose's father John Francis (Honey Fitz) Fitzgerald was a three-term U.S. Congressman who went home to Boston to be elected mayor twice. Joe's father Patrick Joseph (P.J.) Kennedy was a saloonkeeper who invested his profits wisely in banks and real estate and became a state legislator and ward boss. He sent Joe to Boston Latin, the city's most illustrious prep school, and then to Harvard.

P.J. was merely a shrewd and hardworking Irishman. His son was a comet. After college, Joe went on to make a fortune in film production, liquor, real estate and stocks. By the time Franklin D. Roosevelt picked him to be the first chief of the Securities and Exchange Commission, the new regulatory body Roosevelt had formed to police Wall Street, he was a millionaire many times over. But Joe wasn't just a businessman. In the scope of his ambitions and schemes, he was something out of Shakespeare. He married Rose in 1914, and as their children arrived, he formed the conviction not only that the boys belonged in public life but that one of them, maybe more than one, should be President of the United States.

This was the atmosphere that Ted was born into on Feb. 22, 1932—the last of the nine Kennedy children. But from the start, he had three elder brothers as a buffer between himself and the worst of the old man's ambition for his sons. It was enough for a while simply that Teddy, as the baby of the family, made his father feel young again. All the same, he grew up at some distance from his parents. Over the years, Joe and Rose had become increasingly estranged. His father was frequently involved with other women, while his mother consoled herself with trips on her own to Europe. Overweight and lonely, Ted was shuttled through a succession of boarding and day schools. There were 11 by the time he was 14 and enrolled in the last of them, Milton Academy, near Boston.

At Milton, where he would finally have the luxury of being in one place for four consecutive years, Kennedy unexpectedly grew into an athletic, good-looking teenager, one who ambled from there into Harvard, where Jack and Bobby had gone before him. He hadn't been at Harvard long before he screwed up in a way that would come back to haunt him years later. In his freshman year, Kennedy was having trouble with a Spanish class. There was a test coming up, and he needed to do well in order to be eligible to play varsity football the next year. With the encouragement of some of his buddies, Kennedy recruited a friend who was good at Spanish to take the exam in his place. The scheme backfired. The surrogate was caught, and both boys were expelled, though Harvard offered them the opportunity to be readmitted later if they showed evidence of "constructive and responsive citizenship."

Kennedy's abrupt next move was to join the Army, which sent him to Georgia to be trained as a military police officer and then, thanks to his father's intervention, to Paris to serve as an honor guard at NATO headquarters. In the fall of 1953, he was readmitted to Harvard, where he majored in government, got middling grades and in his senior year, with his father and brothers watching from the stands, caught the only touchdown pass of the Harvard-Yale game. Harvard lost 21-7, but Ted earned the varsity letter that had eluded Jack.

After graduation, Kennedy went on to study law at the University of Virginia. He was in law school when he met Joan Bennett, a senior at Manhattanville College, a small Catholic school in New York State that his mother and two of his sisters had attended. Not much more than a year after they first met, they married. Over the next nine years, they had three children: Kara, Edward Jr. and Patrick. (Joan also suffered three miscarriages.) But by 1982, the combination of her prolonged struggle with alcohol and his infidelities led them to divorce. Joan often found herself burdened by the effort required to fill the role of a Kennedy wife. Years later, sounding a bit like Princess Diana, she told an interviewer, "I didn't have a clue what I was getting into."

What she had gotten into was the Kennedys, a family whose family business was politics. Because Joe Jr. had died in World War II, it was Jack who was launched first into public life, winning a Boston congressional seat in 1946 and moving on to the Senate six years later. Ted was still in law school when he was made campaign manager for Jack's 1958 bid for a second term as Senator. Though the real decision-making was left to seasoned Kennedy operatives like Lawrence O'Brien and Kenny O'Donnell, the campaign put Ted in the field constantly to meet and greet voters. It taught him the value of ground-level politicking, the handshakes and legwork that he would need to find it in himself to do all his life.

It also prepared him for a future, coming soon, in which he would be the candidate. When Jack was elected to the White House in 1960, there were four years remaining in his Senate term. The family wanted Ted to succeed him, but at 28, he was two years below the minimum age for the Senate. So a Kennedy loyalist was chosen to fill the seat for a couple of years while Ted used the time to make himself plausible to the state's voters as a man they should send to Washington. With Jack's help, he attached himself to a Senate fact-finding trip to Africa. He toured Latin America, Israel and Berlin. For all that, when he announced his candidacy in March 1962, he still looked to a lot of people like the upstart he was. The editorial page of the New York *Times* called his bid "demeaning to the dignity of the Senate."

But Massachusetts didn't listen to the *Times*. First, Ted handily defeated a Democratic-primary challenger, Eddie McCormack, whose uncle was none other than Speaker of the House John McCormack. Then on Election Day, with 54% of the vote, Kennedy beat George Cabot Lodge in a race that was an ethnic and dynastic grudge match. Lodge was a descendant of the Waspiest of New England political dynasties. His father Henry Cabot Lodge Jr. was

At Robert's home, Hickory Hill, Ted and his brother talk campaign strategies for the 1968 presidential primaries

the incumbent Senator whom J.F.K. had unseated in 1952. His grandfather had been a Senator too and had fought off a challenge in 1916 from Rose Kennedy's father Honey Fitz. But now the venerable Lodges were no match for the Kennedy charm or the Kennedy money.

Knowing that a lot of people saw him as a kid who had ridden into office on his family name, Ted started his Senate career quietly. He took pains to win the sometimes grudging approval of older members with his willingness to learn. "I fully appreciate the wisdom," he once quipped, "of saying freshmen should be seen and not heard."

Ted had been in the Senate for less than a year when J.F.K. went to Dallas the day Lee Harvey Oswald was lying in wait. Jack's death was more than a personal tragedy for Ted. It was a watershed. It put him one step closer to assuming the Kennedy burden, the perennial quest for the heights. It marked the beginning of his transformation into a true public figure.

As a first measure, Ted devoted himself to ensuring the passage of legislation that had been important to his brother, especially the civil rights bill J.F.K. introduced the summer before his death. On June 19, Ted added his vote to the 73-to-27 majority that turned that bill into the historic Civil Rights Act of 1964. Soon after, he headed to the airport to board a private plane that was to take him to the state Democratic Party convention in Springfield, Mass. But as the plane made its descent into a fogbound Springfield airport, it struck a row of trees, then somersaulted across an orchard. The pilot, Ed Zimny, died at the scene. A Kennedy aide, Ed Moss, died a few hours later. Indiana Senator Birch Bayh and his wife Marvella, who were also on board, survived with minor injuries. Kennedy suffered a broken back and a collapsed lung.

What followed was a five-month recovery, mostly spent immobilized in a hospital bed, and a lifetime of back pain, just like his brother Jack's. Yet when he returned to the Senate the following year, Kennedy set to work with the energy that comes to a man who gets a second chance at life. He had already aligned himself with his brother's civil rights legislation. Now he introduced his own Senate bill to ban poll taxes, fees that some Southern states were using to discourage blacks and poor whites from voting. Though his bill was narrowly defeated, the thinking behind it was vindicated the next year when the Supreme Court found the taxes unconstitutional. And it wasn't long before Ted scored a genuine victory on another of Jack's unrealized goals, the reform of immigration quotas to allow more arrivals from nations outside Northern Europe. One year later, he secured federal support for neighborhood clinics, marking the first time he applied himself to the problem of health care, a topic that would become the signature issue of his public life.

By 1967, Kennedy had also begun to speak out against the Vietnam War. Exasperation about Vietnam was one of the main reasons his brother Robert decided to seek the presidency in 1968. Then in June, Bobby was shot down as well. Even more than Jack's death, Bobby's was a blow to Ted. Just six years older, Bobby was the brother Ted had always been closest to. More than that, Bobby's death was a crucial moment of recognition for Ted that the burden of the Kennedy legacy was now his to shoulder. At that time, in the midst of his grief, there also had to be a furious internal discussion within himself of just who he needed to be. For years he had been the Prince Hal of the Kennedy dynasty, the wayward son who would just as soon not inherit the kingdom. But now, at 36, he was the last of the line. There was no one else.

So when Hubert Humphrey lost to Richard Nixon in the fall, Ted instantly became liberalism's last, best hope. There were people who thought he lacked Jack's intellect or Bobby's passion, that all his life he had merely trawled in their wake. But in his first speech after Bobby's death, he was already sounding the cry that would be the great theme of his political life: "Like my brothers before me, I pick up a fallen standard. Sustained by the memory of our priceless years together, I shall try to carry forward that special commitment to justice, to excellence, to courage, that distinguished their lives."

This was the moment when everyone assumed that the presidency would someday be his for the asking. But it was only a moment. On July 18, 1969, Kennedy hosted a reunion for six women who had worked at the center of Bobby's presidential campaign. The gathering took place in a rented cottage on Chappaquiddick Island, just off Martha's Vineyard. Around 11:15 that night, Kennedy asked his driver for the keys to his Oldsmobile so that he could leave the party with Mary Jo Kopechne, a 28-year-old former aide to his brother. According to testimony he gave later at a judge's inquest, he took a wrong turn onto an unlit dirt road and then across a small, unrailed wooden bridge. His car went over the side of the bridge and landed upside down in the water. Kennedy managed to escape. Kopechne did not.

There are questions about Chappaquiddick that have never been closed. Where was Kennedy going with Kopechne at that late hour? (At the inquest in January, he claimed that he was taking her back to her hotel in Edgartown.) Why did he wait until the following morning, 10 hours later, to report the accident to the police? (He said it was because he had been in a state of shock and confusion.) Was the real reason for delaying the report that at the time of the accident he was drunk? (He insisted he was not.) At the inquest, he testified that after escaping from the car, he dived back into the water seven or eight times in a vain attempt to free Kopechne. Then he made the mile-and-a-half walk back to the cottage, where the party was still under way, collected two male friends and returned with them to the car, where they also attempted to free Kopechne. When that proved impossible, Kennedy decided to return to his hotel across the water in Edgartown. But instead of summoning the night ferry, he chose to swim 500 feet across the bay.

The inquest concluded that Kennedy had lied when he said he was taking Kopechne back to Edgartown. It also ruled that his "negligent driving" appeared to have contributed to her death. By the time the inquest was complete, Kennedy had already entered a guilty plea to leaving the scene of an accident and received a two-month suspended sentence. But it would be truer to say he was sentenced to life under the cloud of Chappaquiddick.

The Chappaquiddick "incident" nearly caused Kennedy to leave the Senate. One week after the event, he made a televised speech asking the people of Massachusetts if he should resign. Some 33,000 telegrams poured in telling him to stay on. All the same, the eternal return of Chappaquiddick was enough to derail his presidential ambitions for years. Had it not been for that night, he almost certainly would have been a candidate for the Democratic presidential nomination in 1972. He stayed on the sidelines that year and in 1976 as well, even though in the aftermath of Watergate, that looked to be a winning year for the Democrats. It would be, but for Jimmy Carter.

Kennedy found new issues to throw himself into. In 1970 he introduced his first bill to establish a system of universal health-care coverage. He confounded people who thought of him as a doctrinaire liberal by pushing for airline deregulation and for required sentencing of convicted criminals. He promoted arms-control talks with the Soviet Union but also devoted himself to the cause of Soviet dissidents and would-be Jewish émigrés. He equipped himself with a staff that was the envy of Capitol Hill—for a few years his legal staffer was future Supreme Court Justice Stephen Breyer—but he did his own homework too. He burrowed into the issues he cared about.

It was Chappaquiddick as much as anything else that sabotaged his most serious attempt at the White House: his fight in 1980 to push Carter aside. Almost three decades later, that campaign is still a bit of a puzzle. In many ways, the moment seemed right. When Kennedy came after him, Carter was at a low point in his presidency, which had been hampered for years by double-digit inflation and a weak economy. Then came the coup de grâce of the Iran hostage crisis, which initially helped Carter, as the country rallied around him, but gradually ate away at his standing. When Kennedy first announced his candidacy, some polls showed him with a 2-to-1 lead over Carter among Democrats and independents.

But what exactly, other than a sense that the presidency was a prize that had been denied to him too long, drove Kennedy to run? His ideological differences with Carter never seemed great enough to justify a challenge to a sitting President of his own party. His main complaint was that Carter wasn't moving forward fast enough on health care, "the great unfinished business on the agenda of the Democratic Party," as he called it. It didn't help that in a televised interview on Nov. 4, 1979, just three days before he would launch his campaign, Kennedy gave CBS News correspondent Roger Mudd a notoriously rambling answer to the simple question "Why do you want to be President?" The man who had spent years on a trajectory to the White House still couldn't say exactly why.

In the end, Kennedy won 10 primaries. Carter took 24, then sailed into the propellers of Ronald Reagan in the fall. But that failed campaign liberated Kennedy. He gave the best speech of his life at the 1980 Democratic National Convention, the speech of a man who had no intention of exiting the public stage. Because the White House was never again a serious option for him, he was free to concentrate once and for all on legislating. It was the dawn of the Reagan Revolution, and the Republicans had just retaken the Senate—not an easy time to be the torchbearer for liberalism. But Kennedy assumed the role gladly.

He became not only a dogged defender of the faith but also an even more adept player of the congressional game. In the '80s, he teamed repeatedly with the unlikeliest of allies, conservative Utah Republican Orrin Hatch. It was Hatch and Kennedy who got the first major AIDS legislation passed in 1988, a $1 billion spending measure for treatment, education and research. Two years later, they pushed through the Ryan White CARE Act to assist people with HIV who lack sufficient health-care coverage. But if Kennedy knew how to play ball with the other side, he also knew how to play hardball. When Reagan tried to put Robert Bork on the Supreme Court, it was Kennedy who led the ferocious and ultimately successful liberal opposition.

Kennedy wasn't nearly as prominent in the next major battle over a court seat, the 1991 nomination of Clarence Thomas by George H.W. Bush. Even in the best of times, Kennedy's reputation for womanizing would have made it awkward for him to sit in judgment when Thomas was accused by Anita Hill of sexual harassment. But the Senate hearings on Thomas started at a particularly bad moment for Kennedy, just months after one of the messiest episodes in his public life. In March, while visiting the family compound in Palm Beach, Fla., Kennedy had roused his son Patrick and his nephew William Kennedy Smith out of bed so they could join him for drinks at a local bar. Smith returned to the compound that night with a young woman who would later accuse him of raping her. He was eventually acquitted after a nationally televised trial in which Kennedy was called as a witness. But the image of the capering Senator leading two younger men out to play reawakened all the old misgivings about Kennedy, women and alcohol. The man who had once been Prince Hal, the reluctant heir to the throne, was in danger of turning into Falstaff, the aging reprobate.

Kennedy pulled himself back from that brink. In the summer of the same year, a decade after his divorce from Joan, Kennedy re-encountered Victoria Reggie, a 37-year-old lawyer and gun-safety advocate who had briefly been an intern in his Senate office. Now she lived in Washington with her two children from a previous marriage. Soon they were dating, and a year later they were married. The new marriage transformed Kennedy, giving him a feeling of contentment and stability he had not enjoyed for years. It was a newly energized Kennedy who moved on to the legislative accomplishments of the '90s, like the Family and Medical Leave Act. When the Republicans retook Congress in 1994, it was Kennedy who would push Bill Clinton from the left when Clinton's old soul mates from the Democratic Leadership Council were urging him to move right. "The last thing this country needs," he said then, "is two Republican Parties."

Yet when the next President turned out to be a Republican, Kennedy still found a way to work with him on shared goals. Kennedy spearheaded the effort to pass the No Child Left Behind Act, a priority for George W. Bush. But they later parted ways over what Kennedy felt was Bush's failure to adequately fund the program. And on other issues, there could be no common ground. In 2002, Kennedy was one of the 23 Senators who voted against authorizing the Iraq war. Years later, he would call it the "best vote" he ever cast in the Senate.

But by that time, there had been a lot of good votes—votes that left the country a changed place and a better one. Nobody talks about Camelot anymore. They struck the scenery long ago. Without Ted, the Kennedy legacy would be mostly beautiful afterglow, just mood music and high rhetoric. More than either of his brothers, he took the mythology and shaped it into something real and enduring.

On the weekend of his Inauguration in 1961, John Kennedy gave Ted, the last born of the Kennedy siblings, an engraved cigarette box. It read, "And the last shall be first." That was almost 50 years ago. Neither of them knew then in just what ways that prophecy might turn out to be true.

We do.

Kennedy and his wife Vicki, together on the beach in Hyannis Port, Mass., in 1993

The Kennedys

Sister
Eunice Kennedy Shriver
1921-2009
Eunice created the Special Olympics, which evolved from a summer camp in her backyard

Sister
Rosemary Kennedy
1918-2005
Rosemary, who was developmentally disabled, had an ill-advised lobotomy at 23

Brother
Robert Francis Kennedy
1925-1968
Assassinated while running for President, Bobby was the brother Ted was closest to

Brother
John Fitzgerald Kennedy
1917-1963
Always in Joe Jr.'s shadow growing up, J.F.K. became a war hero, Senator and President

Mother
Rose Fitzgerald Kennedy
1890-1995
The daughter of a popular Boston mayor, Rose raised her sons with a firm hand

Brother
Joseph Patrick Kennedy Jr.
1915-1944
As the eldest, Joe was expected to fulfill his father's dreams but died in World War II

Above, together in the Bronxville, N.Y., house before the war; opposite page, Ted just before turning 2

Sister
Jean Kennedy Smith
1928-
Ambassador to Ireland under Bill Clinton, Jean works for the family's foundations

Edward Moore Kennedy
1932-2009
His brother Jack was his godfather. The youngest of nine, young Ted was both spoiled and teased

Father
Joseph Patrick Kennedy
1888-1969
After making a fortune in liquor, stocks and films, Joe focused on his sons' careers

Sister
Patricia Kennedy Lawford
1924-2006
Once the wife of actor Peter Lawford, Pat was active in her brothers' campaigns

Sister
Kathleen Kennedy Cavendish
1920-1948
The widow of an English marquess, Kathleen died in a plane crash

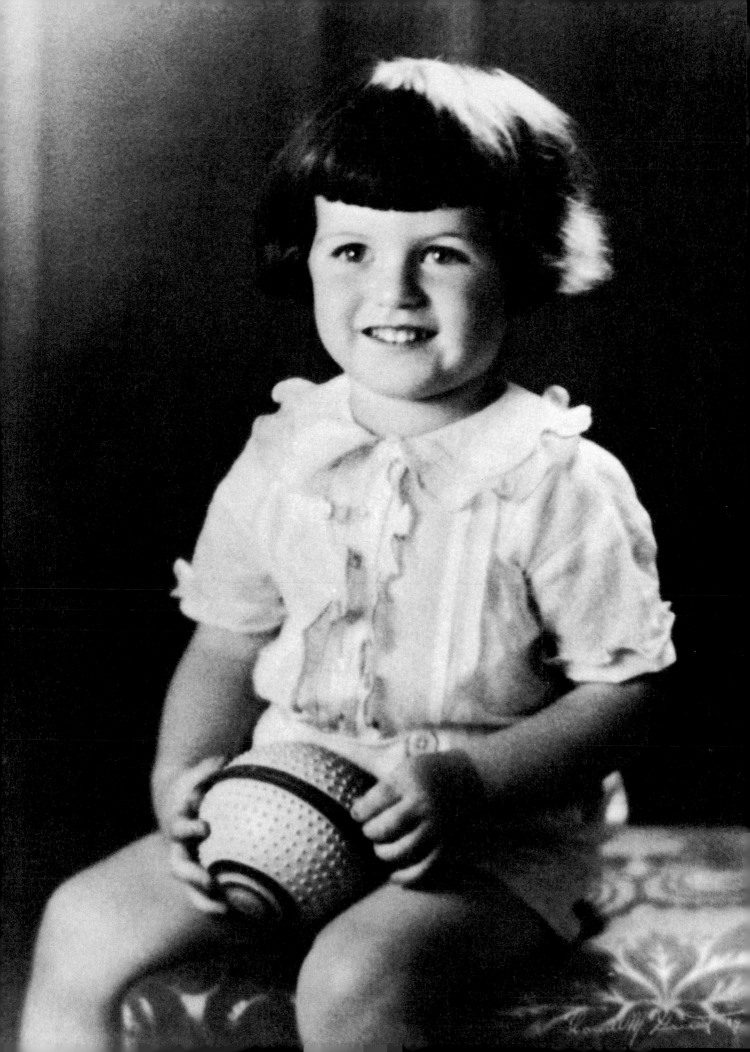

Kennedy warms
up his youngest
child, Patrick, at
Hyannis Port

Ted's Family

First wife
Virginia Joan Bennett
1936-
Nicknamed "the Dish" by Jack, Joan worked as a TV model before marrying into the Kennedy clan in 1958. After a sometimes public battle with alcoholism, she divorced Ted in 1982

Daughter
Kara Anne Kennedy
1960-
Kara, who worked as a news producer in Boston, married architect Michael Allen in 1990 and has two children. She recently battled lung cancer

Son
Edward Moore Kennedy Jr.
1961-
At 12, doctors diagnosed a malignant tumor in Ted Jr.'s right leg, which was amputated above the knee. Now married to Katherine, a psychiatrist, he has two children and runs an asset-management firm

Son
Patrick Joseph Kennedy
1967-
Now serving his eighth term as a member of Congress from Rhode Island, Patrick was just 21 when he was first elected, the youngest Kennedy to take office

Second wife
Victoria Reggie
1954-
Credited with getting Kennedy to live a healthier lifestyle in his later years, Victoria, an attorney, worked in Kennedy's office as a summer intern after college. The two reconnected years later and married in 1992

His Nieces and Nephews

Eunice Shriver's children
Robert; **Maria,** married to Arnold Schwarzenegger, is the first lady of California; **Timothy** is head of the Special Olympics; **Mark** served in the Maryland state legislature from 1995 to 2003; **Anthony** started Best Buddies, a group devoted to the mentally disabled

Patricia Lawford's children
Following in his father's footsteps, **Christopher** became an actor and later published a best-selling memoir about his addictions; **Sydney**; **Victoria**; **Robin**

Robert F. Kennedy's children
Kathleen Townsend, lieutenant governor of Maryland from 1995 to 2003, was the first Kennedy woman to serve in office; **Joseph II** served as a Massachusetts Congressman from 1987 until 1999, when he stepped down to return to nonprofit work; **Robert Jr.** is an environmental activist; **David** died of a drug overdose in 1984; **Courtney**; **Michael** died in a skiing accident in 1997; **Kerry** is a human-rights activist; **Christopher**; **Matthew**; **Douglas** is a journalist; **Rory** is a documentary filmmaker

John F. Kennedy's children
Caroline, the author of at least seven books, serves as president of the J.F.K. Library Foundation and is married to Edwin Schlossberg, who owns a design firm; **John Jr.,** founder of the political magazine *George,* died in a plane crash in 1999 with his wife Carolyn Bessette and her sister Lauren

Jean Smith's children
Stephen Jr. is a lawyer specializing in conflict resolution; **William,** a doctor, was found not guilty in 1991 of raping a woman at the Kennedy estate in Palm Beach, Fla.; **Amanda** wrote and edited *Hostage to Fortune,* letters and biographical essays about Joseph Kennedy Sr.; **Kym**

All in the Family

by ROBERT DALLEK

SEVERAL YEARS AGO, WELL AFTER Ted Kennedy's failed bid to wrest the presidential nomination from Jimmy Carter in 1980, I asked the historian and Kennedy-family confidant Arthur Schlesinger Jr. if he thought the last of the Kennedy brothers could ever win the White House. Only if there was an economic downturn reminding people of the Great Depression, Schlesinger told me, one that renewed enthusiasm for another round of New Deal–style liberalism.

His words reflected the widely shared view that Kennedy had become the heir to Franklin Roosevelt's legacy. And were it not for his age and the collapse of his health, two huge ifs, the 2008 economic meltdown might have been Kennedy's moment—despite Chappaquiddick. All the same, although he couldn't reach for the presidency, he lived long enough to use his considerable influence to anoint Barack Obama as the next heir to the New Deal and also the Kennedy legacy.

Yet by itself Kennedy's standing as the country's most enduring liberal voice was never enough to make him a national icon. After all, liberalism has been in bad odor with a majority of voters at least since Ronald Reagan's election in 1980. Rather, it was Ted's identity as a Kennedy, part of America's royal family, that made him so fascinating to Americans. Forty-six years after John Kennedy was assassinated and 41 years after Bobby was silenced as well by an assassin's bullet, the Kennedy mystique remains a phenomenon.

That mystique begins with Joseph P. Kennedy—the Founding Father, as he's been called, suggesting a comparison to John Adams, Thomas Jefferson, James Madison and George Washington. But the Kennedy legend is of a transparently different order; it's related to the triumph of America's ethnics, the story of how 19th century Irish immigrants acquired wealth, fame and national and international status. It's the Horatio Alger tale writ large—the rise of American newcomers to power and prominence.

Joe Kennedy, like so many other wealthy arrivistes, did not start from the bottom. His father

Ted, at age 7 with Joe Sr. in London, charmed his father with his mischievous antics and sly humor

Patrick Joseph Kennedy—P.J., as he was called—enjoyed a career in the Massachusetts state legislature and as a Boston Democratic Party fixer. His success as a tavern owner afforded his son Joe the opportunity to attend Boston Latin, the city's premier preparatory school, where a handful of aspiring Irish families were allowed to mingle with the offspring of Boston's Brahmins. It opened the way to a Harvard education and the contacts that would launch Joe on his path to great wealth as a banker, Wall Street investor, whiskey importer, Hollywood film mogul and Chicago real estate broker.

Even the economic collapse of the 1930s proved to be more an opportunity than a disaster for Joe, who was something of a financial genius and saw the Crash as a chance to increase his fortune with timely buys of undervalued properties. He also understood the magic of public relations. He seized upon the hard times to make himself and his family famous. In the midst of the Depression, the wealthy Kennedys—Joe, Rose and their nine children—inspired Americans to believe that prosperity remained within reach for their families as well.

The lesson of the Great Depression, Joe told his four sons, was that the next generation of big men in America would be not business titans but political stars—men who could win elective office and use their power to help return the nation to good times. Joe's career path in the '30s echoed his advice to his children. First he accepted an appointment from Roosevelt in 1934 as head of the new Securities and Exchange Commission (SEC), which F.D.R. had established to police the financial industry. When a Roosevelt associate complained to the President about giving a Wall Street insider the chairmanship of the SEC, Roosevelt explained that it takes a thief to catch a thief. Then in 1938, Roosevelt made Joe his ambassador to Great Britain. The ambassadorship was Joe's idea, but it appealed to F.D.R. as a way to twit British conservatives, who would have to deal respectfully with "this redheaded Irishman."

Joe's advice about the importance of politics registered forcefully with Joe Jr., Jack, Bobby and Ted. All four set their sights on political careers. But Joe Jr., the eldest brother and Joe Sr.'s designated candidate for high office—he hoped the highest—perished during a World War II combat mission when his plane exploded over the coast of England. With that, the family's reach for the presidency fell to the second son. Jack had earned a Harvard degree, published a best-selling book on Britain's weak response to Germany before the war and served as commander of a PT boat in the Pacific during World War II, earning a medal for rescuing his boat's crew after a Japanese destroyer sliced it in half. A successful campaign for Congress in 1946 and a victory six years later over incumbent Massachusetts Republican Senator Henry Cabot Lodge gave Jack a launchpad for a presidential run.

Jack's Senate campaign was a Kennedy family affair, with Joe supplying the money, Bobby serving as campaign manager and the Kennedy sisters and 20-year-old Ted helping drum up votes. When Jack ran for the Democratic presidential nomination in 1960, the family again played a large role. In the Wisconsin primary, one observer said, "The family was an asset...genuinely glamorous as well as glamorized, so the people were anxious to meet them wherever they went." Hubert Humphrey, Kennedy's principal opponent, said he felt like a "corner grocer running against a chain store."

Jack struggled against three obstacles to his presidential candidacy. One was his youth. At 43, he would be the youngest man ever elected to the White House. Another was his religion. No Catholic had ever won the presidency, though Al Smith, New York's Catholic governor, had run unsuccessfully for the White House in 1928. The third was his largely hidden health problems: spastic colitis marked by bouts of abdominal pain, diarrhea and dehydration; Addison's disease, an insufficiency of the adrenaline glands that increased the risks of any kind of surgery;

The new ambassador and his family, from left, Kathleen, Ted, Rose, Pat, Jean and Bobby, strolling on the embassy grounds in 1938, became the darlings of the English press

chronic back problems that threatened to make his wheelchair use permanent; and prostatitis and urethritis with periodic infections.

Back surgery in 1954 had brought Jack close to death. But it never dampened his ambition for the presidency. He used his recovery time away from the Senate to work on *Profiles in Courage,* a book about Senators who had risked their political careers to work and vote for national causes larger than themselves. It won a Pulitzer Prize and gave Kennedy greater national visibility in his reach for the Democratic Party's nomination and the subsequent campaign against Vice President Richard Nixon.

Kennedy's victory over Nixon by a scant 118,000 votes, with less than 50% of the popular total, opened the way to a possible dynastic rule of the sort the country had not seen since John Adams and John Quincy Adams became the first father and son to hold the presidency. Jack's appointment of Bobby, who had a law degree from the University of Virginia, as Attorney General and the decision to push Ted into running for Jack's old Senate seat in 1962 raised the unprecedented possibility of brothers succeeding each other in the White House.

The decisions to make Bobby a Cabinet officer and run Ted for the Senate were bold and risky. The Kennedys effectively turned aside any accusations of nepotism with disarming humor. Asked about Bobby's appointment, Jack would joke that he just wanted to give his brother a little legal experience before he practiced law. When a reporter complained to Ted that his election would amount to too many Kennedys in the government, Ted came back, "You should have taken that up with my mother and father."

Within just a few years, of course, Ted was the last surviving Kennedy brother. And his own passing may mark the end of the Kennedy era. No living member of the clan seems likely to replace him as a major influence in national affairs. But Ted's life ended just as forces beyond anyone's control sounded the collapse of Reagan conservatism and the revival of the progressive federal activism Ted saw as essential to a more humane and productive society. The country seems poised to accept a renewed faith in the power of social engineering as essential to the national well-being. The new mood stands as a confirmation of Ted Kennedy's conviction, stated so passionately at the 1980 Democratic Party Convention: "The dream shall not die."

Robert Dallek is the author of An Unfinished Life: John F. Kennedy, 1917-1963

Speaking Out
In May 1971, Kennedy addresses an anti–Vietnam War rally in Washington, where his listeners include future Senator John Kerry, at lower right

Life Goes On

With sister-in-law Ethel, Bobby's widow, as his partner, Kennedy competes in a family match in Hyannis Port in the 1970s

World Traveler
Seen here on a 1974 visit to Yugoslavia's Unknown Soldier Monument, Kennedy was a strong advocate for arms control who went several times to the Soviet Union and Eastern Europe

Supportive Father
**In Moscow in April 1974,
Kennedy walks down a
Kremlin hallway with Ted
Jr., who had recently lost
part of one leg to cancer**

Bus Stop
In September 1974, protesters angered by a court-ordered school-busing plan to integrate Boston schools heckled Kennedy furiously. Some even threw tomatoes

Bowing Out

On Sept. 23, 1974, having decided that a run for President would be too hard on his family, Kennedy announces that he won't be a candidate in the 1976 race. A beaming Joan can't help showing her relief

The Lion of The Senate

by KAREN TUMULTY

WHEN THE PRESIDENT'S BABY BROTHER announced in 1962 that he was running for J.F.K.'s old Senate seat, there was little doubt of the outcome on Election Day. His family machine would make sure of that. But no one supposed he would actually amount to much once he got to Washington. Just three years out of law school, Teddy was the makeweight Kennedy brother. During a televised debate with Massachusetts attorney general Edward McCormack, his opponent in the Democratic primary, McCormack turned to Kennedy and sneered at his thin résumé. "You never worked for a living," he said. Then he turned to the camera: "If his name was Edward Moore, with his qualifications—with your qualifications, Teddy—your candidacy would be a joke. But nobody's laughing, because his name is not Edward Moore. It's Edward Moore Kennedy."

Nearly a half-century later, it's fair to say that of all the Kennedys, Edward Moore was the one who made the greatest impact, the one who did the most to make this a fairer, more just and more compassionate nation. There has not been a major domestic initiative during his time in office that does not bear his stamp: civil rights, education, immigration, workers' rights, health care.

Part of why this Kennedy achieved so much, of course, was that he got what his brothers didn't: longevity. Kennedy served 46 years in the Senate, longer than all but two other men in its history. But the real reason that he is likely to rank alongside Henry Clay and Daniel Webster as one of the greatest legislators to set foot in that chamber has more to do with perseverance. Through 10 Presidents, half of them Republican, Kennedy was the enduring face of liberalism; "to sail against the wind" was one of his favorite metaphors. But how true a course he set for himself.

Kennedy speaks to reporters on Sept. 18, 1962, on the evening of the Massachusetts Democratic primary

schoolchildren could not be taught about evolution, writers and artists would be censored at the whim of [the] government."

The attack was way over the top—so much so that it was initially written off as a serious blunder on Kennedy's part. ("Not one line of that tirade was true," Bork later wrote.) But it stunned the other side and set the terms of engagement for many judicial fights that would follow. As Reagan speechwriter Peggy Noonan put it, acknowledging the deadly effectiveness of Kennedy's assault, "The next time, the Right should answer in kind, matching tone for tone and blow for blow."

Yet when the next of those epic battles over a Supreme Court nominee rolled around—with George H.W. Bush's nomination of Clarence Thomas in 1991—Kennedy was all but silent amid the firestorm over Anita Hill's charges that Thomas had sexually harassed her. That was because it came on the heels of a controversy over his own behavior the previous Easter weekend in Palm Beach, Fla., when he had taken his son and nephew barhopping. The fiasco that grew out of that night, the rape trial of William Kennedy Smith, was the first courtroom spectacle of the cable-television era, and though his nephew was ultimately acquitted, it raised new questions about the Senator's out-of-control personal life. More than two decades after Chappaquiddick, a self-inflicted wound once again threatened to jeopardize everything he stood for.

In October of that year, with a Gallup poll showing his approval rating at 22%, Kennedy made an extraordinary apology before 800 people and a bank of television cameras at Harvard University's John F. Kennedy School of Government. "I am painfully aware that the criticism directed at me in recent months involves far more than honest disagreements with my positions or the usual criticism from the far right. It also involves the disappointment of friends and many others who rely on me to fight the good fight," he said. "To them I say: I recognize my own shortcomings—the faults in the conduct of my private life. I realize that I alone am responsible for them, and I am the one who must confront them." But, he added, "I will continue to fight the good fight."

Indeed, the next years proved to be among the most productive of his career, though he once again found himself sailing into the wind. When his dream of universal health care ran aground with Hillary Clinton's big plan in 1994, he went right back to work in the next session of Congress to try to get there in smaller steps. With Kansas Republican Nancy Kassebaum, he pushed through a bill to limit the ability of insurers to deny coverage to people with pre-existing medical conditions, and he teamed up with Utah's conservative Orrin Hatch, who, despite their differences on just about everything, was one of his closest friends in the Senate, to establish a state insurance program for children. In the same session of partisan bloodletting in which Newt Gingrich shut down the government, Kennedy led a successful fight to raise the minimum wage. He told the New York *Times* that Aug. 2, 1996—when the health-insurance and minimum-wage bills were passed by Congress—was the most satisfying day of his career. "When you know that as a result of legislative change, people's lives are going to be different, and for the better," Kennedy said, "I think you have got something very tangible."

Something far more tangible than a famous last name. In some ways, it felt like the lifting of a burden when he symbolically passed that mantle in 2008. "I love this country. I believe in the bright light of hope and possibility," Kennedy declared in his endorsement of a presidential candidate in whom so many had seen the glimmers of a new Camelot. "I always have, even in the darkest hours. I know what America can achieve. I've seen it. I've lived it." But Ted Kennedy did much more than that. He helped make it happen.

Kennedy arrives at the Capitol for the swearing-in ceremony of President Barack Obama. His impassioned endorsement of Obama early in the 2008 campaign was seen by many as a passing of the Kennedy torch

Party Time

Always the organizer of picnics and other family activities, Kennedy presides over the celebration of his mother's 85th birthday in Hyannis Port in September 1975

Field Trip

To carve out some dedicated family time, Kennedy planned outings like this 1976 expedition to Riverside Amusement Park in Agawam, Mass.

The Home Front

On Nov. 14, 1979, Kennedy and his sister Pat (sitting opposite him) do some early campaigning for the 1980 presidential race at the home of a farm family in Marion, Ohio

Election Fatigue
After a long day of campaigning in Miami in 1979, shortly after announcing his presidential candidacy, Kennedy confers with an aide while his son Patrick and sister Jean doze

Happy Holidays
For their 1978 Christmas portrait, Ted Jr., Joan (holding Patrick), Kara and the Senator gather in their McLean, Va., living room

The Dream Lives On

by BOB SHRUM

LAST SUMMER, AS I flew toward Denver for the Democratic Convention on a small jet with Ted Kennedy, his family and a few friends, I thought of another convention 28 years before. It was the one Kennedy addressed in New York City after losing the Democratic nomination for President to Jimmy Carter. The speech Kennedy hoped to deliver in Denver would echo the earlier one, although a slight change in the closing words would make for a profound shift in mood. The robust Kennedy of 1980, announcing "The dream shall never die" was a young lion in winter, defiant in his beliefs even in defeat. The ailing Kennedy of 2008, stricken with incurable cancer but sailing every afternoon, told me that he was determined to conclude with an affirmation of hope. So the convention and the country would not hear the word die from him. Instead, in that distinctive and commanding voice, he would proclaim, "The dream lives on."

Kennedy delivers his rousing speech at the 1980 Democratic Convention, top; in 2008 he left his hospital bed to urge delegates in Denver to get behind Obama

Ironically, we were thinking of the future in 1980 too, despite the hard reality of our loss. Carter's fortunes had risen in the spring as people rallied behind him when 52 Americans were taken hostage in Iran. He would be doomed by the same crisis when it lasted into the fall, but in the meantime, he invoked it to cancel his one scheduled debate with Kennedy and decline all future ones. Kennedy had surged several times in the long contest. It surprised even us when he trounced Carter in New York. Expecting Kennedy to be defeated, I had originally drafted a statement for him to deliver on the night of that primary that was not just a concession but also a withdrawal from the race. Though the speech wasn't given, its language would be woven into the convention speech two months later.

A speech at the convention would be the only chance in the entire campaign for Kennedy to communicate with Americans in an unmediated way. It was also the last, best chance to make the case for a change in national policies and direction. Kennedy and Carter had deep and principled differences on issues like national health insurance. Kennedy was convinced that unless the party stood for its defining values—and unless Carter at least gave a sense that the next four years could be different—Democrats would be doomed in the fall. We negotiated hard for a speaking slot; Carter's forces were fearful of letting Kennedy anywhere near the podium before a rules vote on Monday sealed the President's renomination. But to deny Kennedy after that would have shattered the convention and the party irrevocably.

What we were conceded was 15 minutes during the debate on the party platform on Tuesday night. At the event, Kennedy took 45, and the applause rolled on for an hour more. He spoke "not to argue as a candidate but to affirm a cause;" and as his voice rang out his vision of change, I watched the delegates, ours and then Carter's, on their feet and on their chairs, swept up in waves of cheering. I had a unique vantage point, sitting on the steps just below the podium, a spot where Kennedy could glance down and see me at any time. He had a superstitious belief—half playful, half serious—that the teleprompter would break, as it had for the hapless governor who placed J.F.K.'s name in nomination at the 1960 convention. If it happened that night, the plan was that Kennedy would look toward me, and I would utter a number to tell him what page of the typed text to turn to.

He delivered a master class that night in taking on Ronald Reagan—not with heavy-handed scaremongering but rather with a light touch that was all the more devastating for its sense of incredulity. "The same Republicans who are talking about preserving the environment have nominated a man who last year made the preposterous statement, and I quote, 'Eighty percent of our air pollution comes from plants and trees.' And that nominee is no friend of the environment." The convention rejoiced as Kennedy arraigned Reagan for a string of similar absurdities; we had discovered in Reagan's past radio shows a previously ignored gold mine of stunning quotes. Kennedy ended the indictment with one of the most far-fetched: "Fascism was really the basis of the New Deal." Then he drove the point home. "And that nominee, whose name is Ronald Reagan, has no right to quote Franklin Delano Roosevelt"—which Reagan did all the time.

The speech was designed as a worded symphony, rising and rousing the audience then falling to a quieter level and aiming to transfix listeners before the tempo picked up again. It was alternately serious and joyful, and it was movingly personal about the individuals and families in trouble whom Kennedy had met on the campaign trail. As he finished, Kennedy, who avoided mentioning his slain brothers in political speeches, now did, but in a carefully understated way, recalling the "words of Tennyson that my brothers quoted and loved, and that have a special meaning for me: 'I am a part of all that I have met;/ ... Tho' much is taken, much abides;

and tho'/ … that which we are, we are;/ One equal temper of heroic hearts,/ … strong in will/ To strive, to seek, to find, and not to yield.'"

You could hear the silence, and I could see people crying across the hall as he finished, "For me a few hours ago, this campaign came to an end. For all those whose cares have been our concern, the work goes on, the cause endures, the hope still lives, and the dream shall never die."

Afterward, Kennedy said to me, "Well, I think it did work." Well enough that by the fall of 1982, he had a better than 3-to-1 lead over Walter Mondale for the '84 Democratic nomination. But within weeks, he announced that he wasn't running—in part, I believe, because he sensed that Reagan was stronger than he seemed and, more decisively, because his children strongly objected to another race. The next time—1988 would be his best chance, I told him, because his opponent would be the first George Bush—he dropped out almost three years before the election. He was convinced that his work in the Senate on issues like sanctions against the apartheid regime in South Africa was being hobbled by the assumption that he was inevitably a presidential candidate. So this time, when he announced that he wasn't, he added something that we had discussed in his living room in Hyannis Port, Mass., a concession that he would never run: "The presidency is not my life; public service is."

So he became one of the greatest Senators of all time and the greatest of his time. He was responsible for more progress than many Presidents. Unlike his brothers, he had the gift of length of years, and how magnificently he used it. He reached across partisan divisions without sacrificing his convictions; he compromised on issues but never ideals. There is in that 1980 speech an insight into the long arc of his achievement: his belief in something bigger than himself, his persistence despite the odds, his capacity to express the conscience of his party and his country's best possibilities. And one other thing: as he also said in that speech, "We have learned to take issues seriously but never to take ourselves too seriously."

I saw it all again on that journey to Denver in 2008. He was taken to a hospital almost as soon as we arrived, was released and then was rushed back again. He was in agony—not from the cancer but from a sudden attack of kidney stones. He was determined to speak to the convention and left his hospital bed just a little more than an hour before his appearance, which much of the press and most delegates regarded as improbable or impossible. I stood and cried as he walked onto the stage. In 1980, he had gone there at the end of a long, hard quest through the primaries. This night was the expression of a lifetime's undiminished commitment, the culmination of three weeks of drafting and daily practice sessions—we live only 25 minutes apart on Cape Cod—and then a harrowing day and a half in Denver. It was courage and conviction about the true purpose of politics that brought him to this moment. He spoke of economic justice, of equality, of health care as a fundamental right, of war and peace. He passed the torch to Barack Obama—to whose candidacy he had given a decisive endorsement the winter before. And he touched millions of hearts one more time: "The work begins anew, the hope rises again, and the dream lives on."

On the plane back to Hyannis, we swapped stories. One was about my cutting the speech in half just hours before he gave it to make it easier for him to get through. He looked at the cuts and teased me, "You took out some of my favorite parts." He laughed, this indomitable man who had given his life to the dream—the dream that in many ways because of him does live on.

A former press secretary and speechwriter for Senator Kennedy, Shrum is now a senior fellow at New York University's Robert F. Wagner Graduate School of Public Service

Strategy Session
During his 1980 presidential run, Kennedy consults with future Kennedy-family biographer Doris Kearns Goodwin, far left, and other advisers, as son Patrick, a future Congressman, looks on

Brother of the Groom
**Ted dances with Jackie
at her wedding to J.F.K.
on Sept. 12, 1953, at
her mother's home in
Newport, R.I.**

Uncle of the Bride
**Caroline asked Ted to
walk her down the aisle
at her Cape Cod wedding
to Edwin Schlossberg on
July 19, 1986**

Reaching Out
Kennedy's visit to apartheid-era South Africa in 1985 convinced him that the U.S. had to put economic pressure on that nation. Once home, he was critical in the push for sanctions

Smooth Sailor

Before she married Kennedy, his second wife Vicki was teasingly warned that she would have to stand in line for her husband's affections behind his boat, *Mya*

The Man Who Found Himself

by Joe Klein

HE SEEMED A GHOST the day I met him. It was Memorial Day, 1970. He was dressed in a black suit, white shirt, black tie. He was still wearing a back brace from the Chappaquiddick accident and he moved stiffly, like a robot cartoon of a politician. He didn't smile, seemed grim even when shaking hands with the civilians; his demeanor was all the more striking because we were at a classic grip-and-grin event, the annual Greek picnic in Lowell, Mass. All sorts of politicians were there, including two who would run for President themselves—Michael Dukakis and Paul Tsongas. The pols gadded about with antic smiles and jackets hooked over their shoulders, ties loosened, sleeves rolled up, trying to look like Kennedys, trying to look ... like him. His family defined political style and vigor for a generation of politicians. But at that moment, and for years after, Ted Kennedy seem to writhe in the public eye.

He was scared catatonic, of course. Scared of death, obviously. There was no reason to believe, in a nation of nutballs, that he would be allowed to continue, unshot. But he was frightened of more profound things as well—overwhelmed by his own humanity in the face of his brothers' immortality, convinced that he'd never measure up, that Joe and Jack and Bobby had been the best of the Kennedys. He was the baby; his political

Kennedy and his wife Joan greet the crowds as they march through South Boston during a St. Patrick's Day parade in 1970

career—the premature ascension to the Senate at the age of 30—was a family conceit, the closest thing to a regency appointment the Senate had ever seen. He was not only the baby, but also the screwup—cheating on his Spanish test in college, boozing and womanizing well beyond the requisite Kennedy-legacy level, and then Chappaquiddick—and even after Chappaquiddick, after he had somehow allowed a young woman to die, they still wanted him to run for President. There was no way to convince them that he was a hollow shell of the dream.

I spent a fair amount of time with him in the 1970s, and most of the circumstances involved pain or awkwardness. I watched him work a supermarket in New Bedford when he ran for re-election in 1976. He accompanied a woman who was shopping for her family. It was total agony. He simply had no idea what to say or do. "So, uh, your family, ah, likes … meat?" he asked. "Oh, yes, Senator," the woman replied, and that was that. No question about the high price of chuck. He stared at her, unable to figure out what came next. Contrary to received wisdom about him, contrary to the joyous Irish bull he later became, he seemed to have no political instincts at all in those days. He went down to Alabama to share a July 4 county-fair stage with George Wallace, another political hologram by then, and Kennedy got smoked. Wallace rose from his wheelchair—a clever series of braces and handles—like the Lord had saved him that very minute, and gave a percussive trumpet solo of a speech, rapid and dexterous and witty. Kennedy read from a text. I was beginning to feel sorry for the guy.

AND NO MORE SO THAN the day we walked through Boston's City Hall Plaza together and got pelted with tomatoes thrown by some of his most loyal and mythic constituents—the aggrieved Celts of South Boston, whose children were about to be bused into a black neighborhood. Afterward, in his office, he offered me a towel to wipe the tomato off my ruined khaki suit and disappeared. But we talked again about that day soon after, and memorably so, since neither of us was sober. It was at a cocktail reception at Ethel Kennedy's home, for recipients of the Robert F. Kennedy journalism awards, one of whom happened to be me. In celebration, before the ceremony, a Kennedy who shall remain nameless took me down to the barn for an intense herbal experience. When I returned to the house, there was Teddy—and it was immediately apparent that he was as shiffazed as I was stoned. We greeted each other like old comrades in arms, sat in a corner and talked about how he wasn't angry about the tomatoes, about how sad and unfair it was that the Irish of Southie and the blacks of Roxbury had to endure busing while the rich kids out in the suburbs got off the hook. It was the first actual conversation we'd ever had. A picture was taken of him handing me the award, which has somehow, sadly, been lost. We were both smiling.

A few months later, I was back at Ethel Kennedy's house—living there as the deputy to Richard Goodwin, the J.F.K. speechwriter who had been tapped as the *Rolling Stone* Washington bureau chief. On July 4 weekend, Hunter Thompson showed up, and I don't remember much else after that, except that a fair number of Ethel's children were involved. Word spread quickly, as word will do in Washington. That Monday, by coincidence, I had an appointment with Kennedy to talk about a story I was working on, and he said, "Joe, before we get started, can I ask you something off the record?" I said sure, and he continued. "What on earth is happening at that house?"

"Why nothing, Senator," I said, summoning all the false gravity in my tiny arsenal. He smiled, raised an eyebrow. "O.K., O.K.," he said. "I asked."

And I was with him the day he was liberated from ambition, finally. It was Feb. 26, 1980, the day of the New Hampshire primary. He was losing—an unimaginable event for a Kennedy, losing in New England. His campaign up to that point had, in fact, been dreadful. He had famously been unable to answer a simple question posed by Roger Mudd of CBS News, "Why do you want to be President?" Because I'm supposed to? Well, that was the truth, but it wasn't an acceptable answer. He had been every bit as shaky and unhappy on the stump as I'd seen him when he ran for Senate. He had blown a 35-point lead. He had been clobbered by Jimmy Carter in Iowa. And now, in New Hampshire, we landed in a small plane and an aide rushed up with the bad news about the early exit polls. He was losing again. "So much for the well-oiled Kennedy machine," he joked, and—I swear—almost immediately became a different person. He gave a looser, more passionate and compelling speech that night. The nomination was clearly lost, but he continued to fight on, stubbornly, disastrously for the Democratic Party, but he actually seemed to be enjoying it, for a change. He gave the speech of his life, "The Dream Will Never Die," at the Democratic Convention that year, and began the far more satisfying Second Act of his life.

THE DEMARCATION WASN'T as clear as all that. He had started becoming an excellent Senator well before his presidential millstone was lifted. He continued, partying way too hard, well after 1980. But the pieces had started to fall into place. He had discovered that, unlike his brothers, he loved the intricacy and camaraderie of the Senate. He became as adept in small rooms, where the deals are made, as his brothers had been on the largest stages. Others can describe his political efficacy, the legislative monuments that will constitute his legacy. For me, the best moments came when we talked about things like returning vets, from Vietnam to Afghanistan—he haunted Walter Reed Army Medical Center, especially whenever a kid from Massachusetts wound up there. I also remember the day when I began to blub as he read the report of a Chilean torture victim, a woman who watched her children be tortured; I pretended not to be blubbing, and he pretended not to notice. If we were women, we might have actually talked about it.

And, speaking of women, Ted Kennedy finally achieved something resembling joy when he met Victoria Reggie. He radiated it, in fact. By the last years, even as he was stooped with weight and hard living, all the signs of awkwardness and discomfort seemed to disappear. He was happy in love, fully engaged in life, proud of his accomplishments. He was, finally, the raucous Irish pol; he began to play with his audiences, acting the old lion, larger than life rather than cowed by it.

We were never friends; our relationship was professional, but keen and, ultimately, affectionate. I don't remember the last time I spoke with him. It might have been in Iowa, during the 2008 campaign—he had the connoisseur's appreciation of Barack Obama. But the last time I saw him that I really remember was a day I stopped by his office to talk about . . . what? Health care, maybe the war in Iraq? His dog was roaming about, rubbing up against me, then settling at the Senator's feet. We were surrounded by his oil paintings of Cape Cod scenes. We talked about his painting; we talked about the Cape, a place we both love, little things—this harbor, that herring run. After all the craziness, after 40 years had slipped between us, he was completely at ease. I wanted to ask him about those awkward, awful times back when. But why mess with the mood? He had exorcised the demons. He was whole.

Wedding Band
**Ted with, from left, Ted Jr.,
John Jr., Patrick and Tim
Shriver, taking a break
from dancing at Ted Jr.'s
Block Island, R.I., wedding
on Oct. 10, 1993**

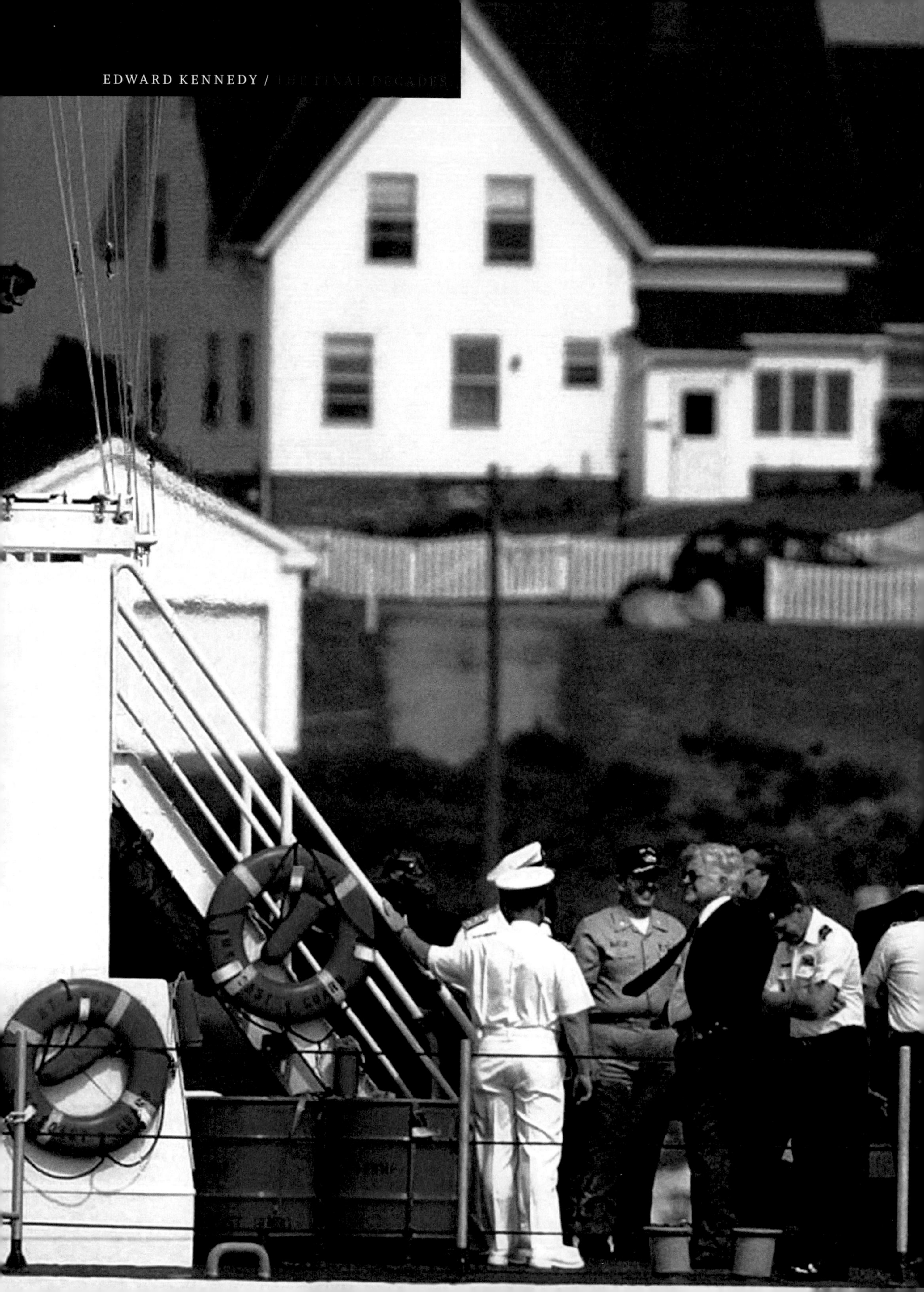

Carrying On
Stepping in as surrogate father, Ted gives a piggyback ride to John Jr. during a ski trip to Stowe, Vt., just four months after his brother's assassination

Heartache
Kennedy returns from the July 22, 1999, dispersal at sea of the ashes of John Jr., his wife Carolyn and her sister Lauren Bessette. They died in a plane crash off the coast of Martha's Vineyard

Crusader

Meeting in Washington with a group of Hispanic broadcasters in May 2007, Kennedy discusses the immigration bill that he co-sponsored with John McCain

"We Shall Prevail"
At a September 2006 rally on the National Mall in Washington, Kennedy promises the crowd that Congress will eventually pass a comprehensive immigration-reform bill

Change Agent

Greeted by a standing ovation from President Barack Obama, left, and son Patrick, third from left, a Rhode Island Congressman, Kennedy grins as he arrives for a White House forum on health-care reform, an issue the Senator supported for more than 40 years.

Hearth And Home

by MIKE BARNICLE

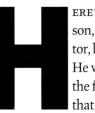

HERE WAS TED KENNEDY, 74-year-old, son, brother, father, husband, Senator, living history, American legend. He was sitting on a wicker chair on the front porch of the seaside home that held so much of his life within its walls. He was wearing a dark blue blazer and a pale blue shirt. He was tieless and tanned on a spectacular October morning in 2006, and he was smiling too because he could see his boat, the *Mya,* perhaps 500 yards in the distance, anchored in Hyannis Port harbor, rocking gently in a warm breeze that held a hint of another summer just passed. Election Day, the last time his fabled name would appear on a ballot, was two weeks away.

"When you're out on the ocean," he was asked that day, "do you ever see your brothers?"

"Sure," Edward Moore Kennedy answered, his voice a few decibels above a whisper. "All the time … all the time. There's not a day I don't think of them.

Kennedy unwinds at the six-acre seaside family compound in Hyannis Port. The Kennedys began spending summers here in 1926

This is where we all grew up. There have been some joyous times here. Difficult times too.

"We all learned to swim here. Learned to sail. I still remember my brother Joe, swimming with him here, before he went off to war. My brother Jack, out on the water with him … I remember it all so well. He lived on the water, fought on the water."

He paused then, staring toward Nantucket Sound as if the cloudless sky of an Indian-summer day somehow held all that he had lost and much of what he remembered. Here, he was not the last living brother from a family that dominated so much of the American political landscape during the second half of the 20th century; he was simply a man who had lived to see dreams die young and yet soldiered on while carrying a cargo of sadness and responsibility.

"The sea … there are eternal aspects to the sea and the ocean," Ted Kennedy said that day. "It anchors you."

He was home. History will focus on his public accomplishments, his Senate career, the burden of burying all his brothers, the lapses of personal judgment, the death by drowning of a young woman, the failed lunge for the presidency, the determination to continue despite staggering trauma. But who he was—who he really was—is rooted in the rambling, white, clapboard house in Hyannis Port to which he could—and would—retreat to recover from all wounds.

HOW OLD WERE YOU WHEN your brother Joe died?" Ted was asked that morning.

"Twelve," he replied. "I was 12 years old."

Joe Kennedy Jr., the oldest of nine children, was the first to die—at 29—when the Navy plane he was flying on a World War II mission exploded over England on Aug. 12, 1944.

"Do you remember the day your family was told?"

"Mother was in the kitchen," he responded right away. "Dad was upstairs. I was right here, right on this porch, when a priest arrived with an Army officer. I remember it quite clearly."

Ted Kennedy remembered it all. The wins, the losses and the fact there were never any tie games in his long life. Nobody was neutral when it came to the man and what he accomplished in the public arena. And few were aware of the private duties he gladly assumed as surrogate father to nieces and nephews who grew up in a fog of myth.

"I wasn't prepared for how his personal pain allowed him to be able to touch and relate to the pain our family felt," Brian Hart of Bedford, Mass., said. "I came to Massachusetts from Texas. I was a conservative Republican. I didn't like what I thought Kennedy stood for, the liberal philosophy. I didn't know the man."

Brian Hart met Ted Kennedy at Arlington National Cemetery on a cold, gray late-October day in 2003. Brian and his wife Alma were burying their 20-year-old son, Army Private First Class John Hart, who had been killed in Iraq. "I turned around at the end of the service, and that was the first time I met Senator Kennedy," the father of the dead soldier said. "He was right there behind us. I asked him if he could meet with me later to talk about how and why our son died—because he did not have the proper equipment to fight a war. He was in a vehicle that was not armored.

"A month later, Senator Kennedy held the first hearing on the need to push the Pentagon to provide more armored humvees for our troops. Later, when I thanked him, he told me it wasn't necessary, that he wanted to thank me for helping focus attention on the issue and that he knew what my wife and I were feeling because his mother—she was a Gold Star Mother too.

"On the first anniversary of John's death, he and his wife Vicki joined Alma and me at Arlington," Brian Hart said. "He told Alma that early morning was the best time to come to Arlington. It was quiet and peaceful, and the crowds wouldn't be there yet. He had flowers for my son's grave. With all that he has to do, he remembered our boy."

Ted Kennedy was all about remembering. He remembered birthdays, christenings and anniversaries. He was present at graduations and funerals. He organized picnics, sailing excursions, sing-alongs at the piano and touch-football games on the lawn. He presided over all things family. He was the navigator for those young Kennedys who sometimes seemed unsure of their direction as life pulled them between relying on reputation and reality.

"When President Kennedy would come here on weekends in the summer, we'd tell the kids that whoever was good during the week would get to ride the helicopter back to Otis on Sunday night," Ted Kennedy remembered, laughing and talking about those summers before Dallas and about Marine One's short flight to Otis Air Base in Falmouth, Mass., a few miles from the family compound.

"God, you should have seen how good those kids would be—Bobby's children, the Shriver kids. They'd get so excited when they'd see that helicopter, all of them jumping up and down. Probably the last time they made their beds and cleaned their rooms."

AN EMOTIONAL MAN, he became deeply devoted to his Catholic faith and his second wife Vicki. Over the last year of his life, he even learned to view the brain cancer that eventually killed him as an odd gift—a gradual fading of a kind that would be easier for his family and friends to come to terms with than the violent and sudden loss of three brothers and a sister, Kathleen. He, at least, was given the gift of time to prepare for the end and to savor memory.

The day after Thanksgiving in 2008, six months after his diagnosis, Ted Kennedy had a party. He and Vicki invited about 100 people to Hyannis Port. Chemotherapy had taken a toll on Ted's strength, but Barack Obama's electoral victory had invigorated him. His children, stepchildren and many of his nieces and nephews were there. So were several of his oldest friends, men who had attended grammar school, college or law school with Kennedy. Family and friends: the ultimate safety net.

Suddenly, Ted Kennedy wanted to sing. And he demanded everyone join him in the parlor, where he sat in a straight-backed chair beside the piano. Most of the tunes were popular when all the ghosts were still alive, still there in the house. Dan Burns, a fourth-grade classmate, sang "Time After Time." Claude Hooten, a law-school classmate, performed "Old Man River." And Ted sang "Some Enchanted Evening," and everyone chimed in, the smiles tinged with a touch of sadness.

The sound spilled out past the porch, into a night made lighter by a full moon whose bright glare bounced off the dark waters of Nantucket Sound, beyond the old house where Teddy—and he was always "Teddy" here—mouthed the lyrics to every song, sitting, smiling, happy to be surrounded by family and friends in a place where he could hear and remember it all. And as he sang, his blue eyes sparkled with life, and for the moment it seemed as if one of his deeply felt beliefs—"that we will all meet again, don't know where, don't know when"—was nothing other than true.

"I love living here," Ted Kennedy once said. "And I believe in the Resurrection."

Mike Barnicle was a columnist at the Boston Globe *for 25 years*